# AN ADVENT DEVOTIONAL

*for the* _____ FAMILY

_____
*date*

D1530186

A Family Devotional to Help You Celebrate Jesus

# The 25 DAYS of CHRISTMAS

JAMES MERRITT • Illustrated by Connie Gabbert

HARVEST HOUSE PUBLISHERS

Eugene, Oregon

Unless otherwise indicated, all Scripture quotations are from The ESV® Bible (The Holy Bible, English Standard Version®), copyright © 2001 by Crossway, a publishing ministry of Good News Publishers. Used by permission. All rights reserved.

Verses marked NLT are taken from the Holy Bible, New Living Translation, copyright © 1996, 2004, 2015 by Tyndale House Foundation. Used by permission of Tyndale House Publishers, Inc., Carol Stream, Illinois 60188. All rights reserved.

Verses marked TLB are taken from The Living Bible, copyright © 1971. Used by permission of Tyndale House Publishers, Inc., Carol Stream, Illinois 60188. All rights reserved.

Cover design and interior design by Connie Gabbert
Published in association with the Christopher Ferebee Agency

THE 25 DAYS OF CHRISTMAS
Copyright © 2018 by James Merritt

Published by
HARVEST HOUSE PUBLISHERS
Eugene, Oregon 97408
www.harvesthousepublishers.com

ISBN 978-0-7369-7310-6 (hardcover)
ISBN 978-0-7369-7311-3 (eBook)

Library of Congress Cataloging-in-Publication Data
Names: Merritt, James Gregory, 1952- author.
Title: The 25 days of Christmas / James Merritt ; illustrated by Connie Gabbert.
Other titles: Twenty-five days of Christmas
Description: Eugene : Harvest House Publishers, 2018.
Identifiers: LCCN 2017055253 (print) | LCCN 2018005428 (ebook)
ISBN 9780736973113 (ebook) | ISBN 9780736973106 (hardcover)
Subjects: LCSH: Christma—Prayers and devotions. | Families—Religious life.
Classification: LCC BV45 (ebook) | LCC BV45 .M443 2018 (print)
DDC 242/.335—dc23
LC record available at https://lccn.loc.gov/2017055253

**All rights reserved.** No part of this publication may be reproduced, stored in a retrieval system, or transmitted in any form or by any means—electronic, mechanical, digital, photocopy, recording, or any other—except for brief quotations in printed reviews, without the prior permission of the publisher.

**Printed in China**

19 20 21 22 23 24 25 26 / RDS / 10 9 8 7 6 5 4 3 2

LET'S

*Celebrate Jesus...*

THE LIGHT OF THE WORLD

*Today we begin* our journey to Christmas. There's so much more in store than we ever imagined. It's an adventure. It's a history of the mystery of eternity. This is the amazing story about why Jesus was born so many years ago and how he lives in us today.

For 25 days we will gather the treasures of the season to carry with us forever.
This is the way Christmas was meant to be experienced!

- *Light up* our days with joy.
- *Decorate* our hearts with God's hope.
- *Sing* our praises to the newborn King.
- *Believe* in the birth of a Savior.

- *Create* family memories.
- *Wrap* our spirits in God's word.
- *Receive* the ultimate gift.
- *Give* the love of Christ to others.

Are you ready?
Let's journey to Jesus.
He's the baby in the manger
and the Lord of our lives.

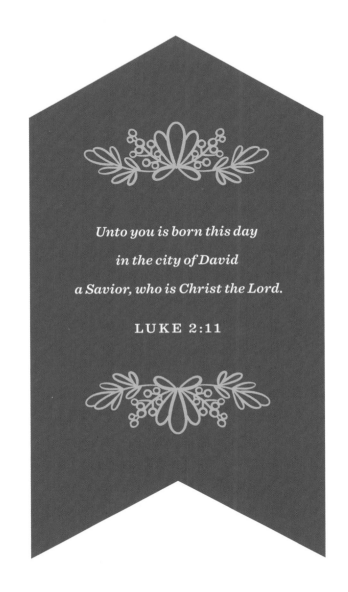

*Unto you is born this day*

*in the city of David*

*a Savior, who is Christ the Lord.*

LUKE 2:11

# Contents

# Christmas in the Garden

GENESIS 3:1-15

***Santa Claus, Rudolph,*** Jack Frost, the Grinch, Ebenezer Scrooge—all of these stories have become part of our modern celebration of Christmas. But most people, even those who don't go to church regularly, could probably tell you that none of these is the *real* story of Christmas. Everyone knows that the Christmas story started 2000 years ago with the birth of Jesus, right? Actually, no! The story of Christmas actually starts at the beginning of the first book of the Bible, at the very beginning of human history, in a place about as far removed from our idea of a cozy and snowy Christmas setting as possible. The story of Christmas begins in a garden.

The Garden of Eden was as close to heaven on earth as a place could possibly be. The weather was perfect, the flowers never withered, and if there were wasps, they never stung anyone. Adam and Eve didn't have to worry about hunger or animal attacks or splinters. They were at perfect peace with each other, and God even walked with them in the garden.

But something happened that plunged this perfect world into the conflict that still rages today, something that causes all the suffering on the planet. The first sin was committed. You may think of sin as breaking a rule, but as we see in the Eden story, sin is simply disbelieving God's word and disobeying his will. From the moment Eve disbelieved and disobeyed, everything and everyone has been infected by sin. Roses have thorns. Airports need metal detectors. Cities need cemeteries. And sin has poisoned more than the world around us. Why do we do things we know we shouldn't, and why don't we do what we know we should? Something is wrong in our hearts.

But God never leaves a problem unsolved. In the same moment sin entered the world, God had the solution ready, and he revealed it almost immediately in a single verse holding hope for the entire world. "I will put enmity between you and the woman, and between your offspring and her offspring; he shall bruise your head, and you shall bruise his heel" (Genesis 3:15). The serpent would bruise the heel of this Savior, but the Savior would trample the head of the serpent. You don't have to be a doctor to know which injury is worse—a bite to the foot or a kick to the head! Sin was to be defeated. We were to be rescued.

You may never have heard this verse referred to as the first Christmas story, but that's exactly what it is. It's the very first verse in the Bible to tell of a Savior who would bring us salvation from our sin. The most familiar Christmas verse in the Bible is probably Luke 2:11: "For unto you is born this day in the city of David a Savior, who is Christ the Lord." The very first word used to describe the newborn baby is "Savior" because that is what the world had been waiting for all those long years since Eve ate the fruit. Only when we understand our need for a Savior can we fully experience the celebration of his birth. So with every Christmas movie we watch, every cookie we bake, every carol we sing, and every decoration we hang, let these words echo: "I need a Savior—and he is here!"

*Father God, thank you for solving the problem of our sin so we could once more walk with you. Thank you for sending us a Savior, and help us to remember our need for him every day of this Christmas season. Amen.*

## Celebrate

Write "I need a Savior, and he is here!" on some index cards. Parents or older children can print them, and younger children can decorate them. Put these notes where you'll find them as the Christmas season unfolds—filed with the Christmas cookie recipes, stored with the gift wrapping supplies, and tucked in the cases of your favorite Christmas CDs or DVDs. As you enjoy your favorite Christmas activities, you'll find these reminders of the reason behind all the fun and celebration.

# What Child Is This?

### ISAIAH 9:6-7

*In 1865, as Christmas* was approaching, an insurance salesman named William Chatterton Dix wrote a poem he called "The Manger Throne." Dix imagined that those who passed by the manger 2000 years ago might have been confused about who the child was who lay before them. Why was he in a feedbox? Why were shepherds worshipping him? Why were angels singing over him? Part of the poem was set to a traditional English melody, and it eventually became the well-loved Christmas song "What Child Is This?"

The world has been asking that question and debating the answer for the past 2000 years. Muslims, for example, believe that Jesus was born of a virgin just as Christians do, but they see him only as a great prophet, not as God. Many Jewish people now see Jesus as a great teacher and political activist but not the Messiah. Buddhists see him as a perfectly enlightened being, full of compassion, who helps others. And millions of people who don't embrace any particular religion don't know what they think about him. So the question remains, what child is this? Well, 700 years before Jesus was born—before the star shone, the shepherds knelt, and the angels sang—a prophet of God named Isaiah told us in no uncertain terms exactly who this child was.

Jesus would come to be known by many names and titles—Lord, Savior, Christ, King of Kings, the Lion of Judah, the Rose of Sharon—but Isaiah gives us four special names that tell us specifically what Jesus would be to *us*. To the hurting and confused, Jesus is the Wonderful Counselor. Isaiah 28:29 says, "The Lord of hosts…is wonderful in counsel and excellent in wisdom." Unlike human counselors, Jesus doesn't give advice or opinions—He gives truth. He *is* the truth (John 14:6). The greatest counselor you can ever have is the Son of God; the greatest counsel you will ever find is in the word of God.

To the helpless, Jesus is the Mighty God. Present everywhere, limitless in power, with nothing hidden from his knowledge, he is an ever-present help (Psalm 46:1). Nothing is impossible with this Mighty God. To the orphan and the lonely, Jesus is the Everlasting Father, a Father who will never leave or forsake you, who was before all things and will outlast all things, and who knew your name from before the foundations of the earth. And to the hopeless and weary, Jesus is the Prince of Peace. The peace he gives is not like the peace the world gives, which depends on fragile treaties and temporary solutions. Jesus gives perfect peace that can weather any storm.

Someday, the whole world will no longer have to ask, "What child is this?" The child who was laid in a manger will sit on a throne. The babe worshipped by shepherds will be worshipped by kings and rulers. And of the reign of this Wonderful Counselor, Mighty God, Everlasting Father, and Prince of Peace, there will be no end.

*Everlasting Father, thank you for loving us before the beginning of time. Mighty God, thank you for being our helper and our defender. Wonderful Counselor, thank you for giving us your word to guide us. And Prince of Peace, help us to share your peace with those around us this Christmas. Amen.*

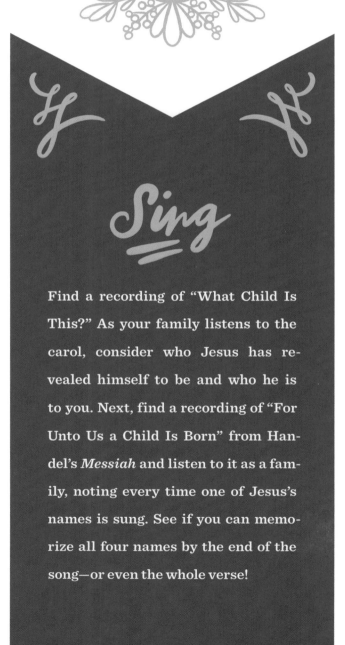

## Sing

Find a recording of "What Child Is This?" As your family listens to the carol, consider who Jesus has revealed himself to be and who he is to you. Next, find a recording of "For Unto Us a Child Is Born" from Handel's *Messiah* and listen to it as a family, noting every time one of Jesus's names is sung. See if you can memorize all four names by the end of the song—or even the whole verse!

# The Masterpiece

## MATTHEW 1:1-17; LUKE 3:23-38

**When reading the book** of Matthew or Luke, it's tempting to skip over the long lists of names found in the early chapters. After reading three or four names into one of these lists, you may feel your eyes start to glaze over. *Get to the good part,* you may be thinking! These long family trees may not seem as interesting as the familiar stories about the shepherds and the wise men, but every word of the Bible is from God, so if he thought it was important for us to know who was in Jesus's family tree, we need to pay attention.

To understand why the genealogies listed in Matthew and Luke are important, think of the story of Jesus as you would a huge painting or mosaic—a masterpiece by a master artist, like the ceiling of the Sistine Chapel in Vatican City. Michelangelo took four years to complete the huge work, and only when viewed from a distance, from the floor of the chapel, can the scale and scope of the full work be appreciated. In the same way, when we look at the big picture of Christmas, we can appreciate the thousands of years and millions of tiny brushstrokes God used to complete the masterpiece of the birth of Christ.

Matthew presents Jesus as the Messiah, a figure the Jews had been told would be a king. Unlike a president, a king does not come to rule by ballot, but by birth. A king has to prove his right to the throne by proving he is descended from the royal family. God had revealed that the Messiah's "right to rule" would be proven by three things: He would come from the family of Abraham (Genesis 22:18), he would come from the tribe of Judah (Genesis 49:10), and he would come from the house of David (2 Samuel 7:12-13). Now you see why God thought it was important for us to see these names in Jesus's family tree—they demonstrate his legal right to the throne.

But the genealogies reveal even more than that. Jesus's legal right to rule came through Joseph, but the Bible makes clear that the Messiah would be a descendant of David. As Joseph's adopted son, Jesus was a legal descendant but not a descendant of David by birth. Just so there would be no doubt at all about Jesus's claim to the throne, God told Luke to include the other side of his genealogy—his mother's side—which can also be traced back to David through one of his other sons. Jesus was physically born of Mary, so her genealogy shows us that he was a literal descendant of David as well as a legal descendant.

God didn't leave one square inch of his canvas unfinished. He didn't use one brushstroke too many or too few, but just the right strokes and just the right colors to create the masterpiece of the birth of Christ.

*Dear Father, thank you for being the master artist who arranges our lives the same way you arranged Jesus's claim to his throne. Help us to trust that you are always working to place us exactly where you want us in the masterpiece you're creating.*

Draw

Decide as a family on the subject for a group art project. Pick a simple object or animal whose parts can be assigned to the members of the family. For example, an elephant can be divided into tail, body, trunk, and ears. A tree can be divided into branches, trunk, roots, leaves, and fruit. Decide who is going to draw or paint each part of the picture, but don't discuss any other details about the picture, such as how big it will be or what color it will be. On separate pieces of paper, everyone draws or paints their individual part of the picture. When everyone is finished, try to assemble your picture using all the separate pieces to make the whole.

How did you do? You might have created a pretty decent picture of your object, or you might have created a monster! What does this exercise teach us about the "big picture" of our lives?

# Jesus's Family Tree

MATTHEW 1:3-6

***Have you ever examined*** your family tree? A family tree is a diagram that shows all the individuals who make up your family, from your great-great-great-great-grandparents all the way to you. Some people love to research their family tree because they like to find out where they came from and who they're related to. It can be especially fun to discover that you're distantly related to a famous person from history, like George Washington or Thomas Edison!

You might think Jesus's family tree would be full of some of the wisest, most influential, and most righteous people who ever lived. But the truth is, Jesus's family tree has quite a few names on it that we wouldn't necessarily want to brag about having

in our family. Abraham was a liar who pretended his wife was his sister. Jacob was a cheater who stole his brother's birthright. And though David was a king, he was also an adulterer and a murderer. Perhaps the most surprising person to appear on Jesus's family tree, however, is Rahab, David's great-great-grandmother.

In Jesus's time, Jewish culture didn't regard women very highly, so it's surprising that Rahab is mentioned in Jesus's genealogy at all. We might conclude that she was an exceptionally righteous or humble person to be Jesus's ancestor and mentioned by name in his family tree, but when we read her story, we find out that she was not only a Canaanite—an enemy of the Israelites and an idolater—but also a woman with a very bad reputation. Respectable society wouldn't have had anything to do with this woman, yet God changed her heart, changed her life, and included her in his master plan. He gave her an important part to play in giving the Promised Land to his people, and he even included her in his own Son's family tree.

None of the names in the first chapter of Matthew are there by accident. God guided the marriages and births that had to take place through the centuries to form Jesus's family tree, and every person in his lineage was handpicked by God to be part of it.

I'm willing to bet that most of those people had no idea during their lifetimes of the way God was using them in his much bigger plan to save the world. That's an important truth for us to remember—our lives might seem obscure or unimportant or broken or sinful, but God can use every person who's ever been born and fit us exactly where he wants us to be in his plan for the world.

*Lord, thank you for the reminder*
*that you are willing to use any of us,*
*regardless of the mistakes we've made or*
*the way we've messed up in the past,*
*as long as we are available to you.*
*Help us to see the ways you want to use*
*us this Christmas, and give us grace*
*to be obedient to your leading. Amen.*

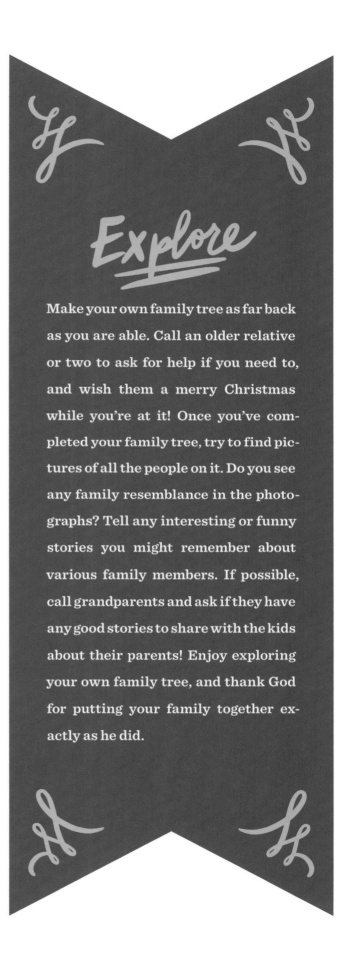

## Explore

Make your own family tree as far back as you are able. Call an older relative or two to ask for help if you need to, and wish them a merry Christmas while you're at it! Once you've completed your family tree, try to find pictures of all the people on it. Do you see any family resemblance in the photographs? Tell any interesting or funny stories you might remember about various family members. If possible, call grandparents and ask if they have any good stories to share with the kids about their parents! Enjoy exploring your own family tree, and thank God for putting your family together exactly as he did.

# The Waiting Room

***Sitting in a hospital*** waiting room is no fun. Not knowing what the doctor will say, not knowing whether the cancer is back, not knowing if the operation was successful…these are difficult situations.

You may find yourselves in other "waiting rooms" too—waiting for a job, waiting to meet someone to spend the rest of your life with, or waiting for enough money to pay the rent. If you've ever found yourself in one of these waiting rooms, you know what the Jewish people had been feeling like for hundreds of years before Jesus was born.

Lots of children today hear the story of Santa Claus and wait anxiously for him to bring gifts on Christmas Eve, but for thousands of years, children in Jewish families were told a true story far more wonderful and awe-inspiring. They learned that God would one day send a Messiah, a Deliverer, someone who would rule over the entire world. They waited anxiously for him, but as the centuries passed and the Jewish people were subjected to captivity, foreign rule, and persecution, no Messiah appeared. Now, just before the birth of Christ, they'd been sitting in the waiting room for 400 years without even a whisper from God—no prophecies, no miracles, nothing.

Zechariah and Elizabeth had been in their own waiting room throughout their marriage. For decades they had prayed that God would bless them with a child, and for decades their arms and Elizabeth's womb had remained empty. Zechariah and Elizabeth probably felt a lot like the nation of

Israel—weary of praying, losing hope that God would respond, wondering if he was even listening—when an angel suddenly showed up in the waiting room.

"Your prayer has been heard," the angel said. If you've ever felt as if your prayers were being spoken to an empty room, you know how encouraged Zechariah must have been when he discovered that God had been listening to every word. What's more, God had not been idle or forgetful during those years of silence. God had marked the birthday of Zechariah's child on his calendar before Elizabeth and Zechariah were married…before they were even born! Throughout their long years of praying, he had been moving in the events of the world to bring Zechariah, Elizabeth, Joseph, Mary, Caesar Augustus, and the nation of Israel to this exact point in time when everything would align for his plan of salvation to be set into motion.

Even when you feel as if you've been in the waiting room forever or God has forgotten all about you, Zechariah and Elizabeth's story shows that while we are waiting, God is moving. During those 400 years of silence, when the Jews were tempted to lose faith that a Messiah would ever come, God had already made and confirmed his reservations for his time on earth. His arrival date was on the calendar before the creation of the world. Christmas proves that God never forgets his promises and always keep his appointments. So no matter how long you've been in the waiting room, keep watching—God is coming!

*Lord Jesus, thank you for your perfect timing at the first Christmas and in each of our lives. Help us to trust that when you seem to be silent, you're still working to accomplish your purpose in our lives. Give us patience when we're in the waiting room, and thank you that we have Christmas as a reminder that you came once and are coming again. Amen.*

## Play

Play a family game that includes a timer, such as Catch Phrase, Boggle, or Scattergories. Notice the excitement you feel when the timer is started. How does "God's timer" help you when you're waiting for his plan to unfold?

# Timing Is Everything

## GALATIANS 4:4

*Hitting a baseball* has been described as the most difficult feat in all of sports. I played baseball, and I believe it! It takes incredible hand-eye coordination to swing a piece of wood three inches wide at a little white ball traveling 95 miles an hour. If you manage to connect ball to bat, a difference in timing of *a hundredth of a second* can determine whether a hit will be a foul ball or a 400-foot home run. Timing is everything in baseball.

Have you ever wondered about the timing of Christmas? Why was Jesus born when he was? Why didn't he come much earlier? Why did God wait around for thousands of years before sending Jesus onto the scene? The apostle Paul answers those questions with a simple statement about Christmas,

one that would be easy to miss if you weren't looking for it: "When the fullness of time had come, God sent forth his Son" (Galatians 4:4).

The phrase "fullness of time" comes from a Greek expression loaded with meaning. It describes something that is completely and fully developed, like a ripe apple that is ready to be picked or a pregnant woman who is ready to deliver her baby. It refers to a time appointed in advance for something to happen. According to Paul, the birth of Jesus came at the exact moment when everything was in place, when everything was perfectly lined up and the stage was perfectly set.

If we walk down the road of history a little way, we can see why God's timing of Jesus's birth was so perfect. Three hundred fifty years before Jesus was born, a Greek named Alexander the Great set out to conquer the known world. In 12 years, he had done just that. Because of Alexander's conquest, the world adopted a universal language—Greek, which was still common during Jesus's earthly ministry.

When the Romans defeated the Greeks, they used their wealth to build roads patrolled by soldiers, and that allowed for relatively safe travel throughout the empire. The most efficient postal system in existence at the time allowed letters to be written and dispatched all over the known world. Into this time in history, when most of the civilized world was within reach, the Savior of the world was born. The time was just right for the good news of the Messiah to spread like wildfire. Less than a generation after Jesus's crucifixion, the early disciples had carried his story to every country in the Roman Empire. Within three centuries, Christianity was the official religion of the empire.

In the fullness of time, God sent his Son to a world desperate for a Savior. Just as there was an exact time for Jesus to be born, there is an exact time when he will come again, so the exact time for us to put our faith in him is now.

*God, thank you for sending your Son to earth at just the right time. Thank you for never being too early or too late. Help us to trust your perfect timing in our lives when we feel impatient or anxious. Amen.*

# Create

Make a family timeline. Start with the birthdate of the oldest person in your immediate family and add as many significant events as you can—other birthdates, vacations, moves, graduations, job changes, losses you may have suffered, major world events, changes in technology, and so on. If you want too, look up the birth year of each family member and read a few of the biggest headlines from that year.

How would your lives have been different if you were born even a little sooner or later? Thank God for working out the timing of your lives just right so you can enjoy your life, your family, and your friends.

# Believe and Say Yes

**Without question,** the most famous mother in history is Mary the mother of Jesus. She has been the subject of countless paintings and sculptures and songs. More little girls have been named after her than after any other woman who has ever lived.

Mary was the only person who was present at both the birth of Christ and his crucifixion. She saw Jesus enter the world as her son and leave as her Savior. Without a doubt, Mary's job was one of the most special and most sacred of any that God has ever given to anyone, so naturally, people have spent a lot of time trying to figure out exactly why God picked Mary for the honor of being Jesus's mother. Nowhere does the Bible say she was per-

fect or sinless. Nowhere does it say she was God or equal with God. And yet out of the whole world, God chose this poor, undistinguished peasant girl from a nondescript city to be the mother of Jesus.

If there was anything extraordinary about this ordinary Jewish girl, something that would explain why God chose her for this role, it was her immediate response to the incredible things the angel told her: "I am the Lord's servant. May everything you have said about me come true" (Luke 1:38 NLT). Mary knew her life was going to look different from what she had expected. She probably guessed she would encounter gossip and scorn when she was found to be pregnant. Yet when she learns what God's will is for her, Mary simply believes and says yes.

Christmas has a lot to do with God's promises. He promised Adam and Eve that their offspring would overcome evil. He promised Isaiah that a virgin would conceive and bear a son. He promised Mary that she would conceive and give birth to the Savior. Evidently, God wants us to know without a doubt that he keeps his promises. The angel even affirms that "every promise from God shall surely come true" (Luke 1:37 TLB). Why then do we continue to live as if we're not sure whether God can be trusted? Why do we hesitate to believe his promises and to follow his will when it's revealed?

Though he may not send angels with personalized instructions very often, God has a custom plan for every one of us, a purpose he wants each of us to fulfill. God didn't choose Mary because she was smart or sinless or talented, and those aren't the reasons he chooses us. Rather, he uses ordinary people who believe his promises and act as if they are true, following his will even when it seems unpleasant, difficult, or even dangerous. Mary's cousin Elizabeth says, "You are blessed because you believed that the Lord would do what he said" (Luke 1:45 NLT). Like Mary, we can be used in extraordinary ways if our response to God is to believe and say yes.

*Jesus, help us to be like Mary, to be open to hearing your will. Make us ready to believe and say yes when you speak to us. Thank you for all the times you've kept your promises to us. Amen.*

## Connect

Throughout history, people have done some amazing things simply because they believed and said yes to God. Noah built an ark—and saved the human race. Abraham moved his household hundreds of miles—and inherited the Promised Land. Moses led Israel out of slavery, young David defeated a giant, and Peter walked on water...because they believed and said yes.

Take turns sharing one way your life has changed because you have believed God and said yes to him.

# Magnify

***One thing that makes*** the Christmas season stand out from every other holiday celebration is the music. Think about it—you don't hear Labor Day music playing in the mall in early September. The radio doesn't play Thanksgiving music 24/7 in November. People don't go door-to-door singing patriotic songs on Independence Day. Yet for more than a month before Christmas, wherever you go from morning to night, you can bet you'll hear Christmas music!

Unlike some Scrooges, I love Christmas music—because God loves it! The birth of his Son was announced and celebrated with music right from the time Jesus was conceived. And the person who wrote and sang the very first Christmas song was none other than Jesus's mother, Mary.

We hear Mary's song when she sings it to her cousin Elizabeth, the mother of the yet-to-be-born John the Baptist. It's become known as the Magnificat (the Latin word for "magnify") because of the first line of the song: "My soul magnifies the Lord." This one line sums up the state of Mary's heart as she considers what the angel told her and the part she will play in God's plan to redeem the world. Far from becoming conceited or proud about her role as the mother of the Messiah, Mary is humbled and awed by God's goodness to her, his mercy to those who fear him, and the promises he has kept to his people. Her very soul is crying out for God to be magnified—to be made great, to be praised, to be elevated to the highest level.

It only makes sense that if Christmas is the celebration of the birth of Christ, then he ought to be magnified during the season, the subject of every song, the reason for every party. I probably don't have to tell you that the exact opposite usually happens in our Christmas culture. More and more, Christ is not magnified. He is minimized, pushed aside to make way for Frosty and Rudolph, drowned out by songs about winter wonderlands and roasting chestnuts. All too often, not only is Jesus not magnified in our celebrations, but you couldn't find him with a magnifying glass!

Many of the people you work with, go to school with, or live next door to believe that Jesus Christ is simply not that important. He's very small in many lives in comparison to other things and other people, and he seems very far away and long ago. That is why you and I must be magnifiers of Christ, like Mary. We need to praise him with our words. We need to elevate him in the way we live, in the kindness we show, and the love we share. At Christmas, and all year long, let us magnify him.

*Jesus, teach us how to magnify you with our words, just as Mary did. Teach us how to give you a bigger place in our Christmas celebrations and in our lives, and let us act as magnifying glasses to better show you to the world. Amen.*

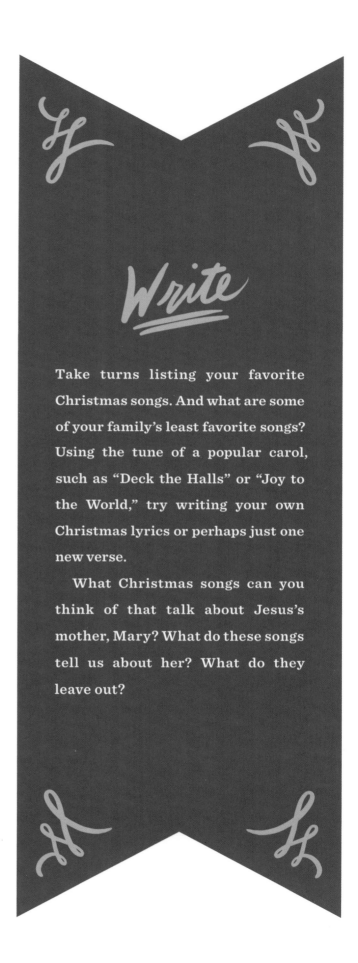

# Write

Take turns listing your favorite Christmas songs. And what are some of your family's least favorite songs? Using the tune of a popular carol, such as "Deck the Halls" or "Joy to the World," try writing your own Christmas lyrics or perhaps just one new verse.

What Christmas songs can you think of that talk about Jesus's mother, Mary? What do these songs tell us about her? What do they leave out?

# A Man of Few Words

MATTHEW 1:18-25; 2:13-23

***Every year at Christmas,*** we hear a lot about many characters in the Christmas story. We hear about Mary and the shepherds, we hear about the wise men and even the donkey, but one character always seems to be tagging along, a player in the scene but without any lines. Any guesses as to whom I'm talking about? If you said Joseph, you're right! Compared to the rest of the figures in our nativity scene, Joseph seems kind of dull. He doesn't sing any songs or bring any gifts—he just stands there in his sandals and his robe, minding his own business.

This picture of Joseph doesn't tell the whole story, however. Though we don't hear much about the part Joseph played on the night of the birth of Christ, his faith allowed God to use him in some pretty signif-

icant ways both before and after Jesus was born. You might say Joseph was a man of few words but great acts of faith.

First, we know it wasn't an accident that Joseph ended up as Jesus's earthly father. God used him to fulfill the promise that the Messiah would be a king from the line of David. Of course, Joseph didn't get to choose his ancestors, so why should he get any credit here? Well, Joseph *did* have to choose whether he would be Jesus's adoptive father. He could have doubted the dream in which an angel of the Lord spoke to him. Or he could have believed but chosen to walk away from Mary, not wanting to take on the drama of a pregnant fiancée and a baby Messiah. But he didn't doubt, and he didn't turn his back on the woman and the baby God had entrusted to him. Instead, he believed God's promise and acted in faith, accepting the responsibility God had offered him to be the adoptive father of the Messiah.

And Joseph wasn't done with great acts of faith. Again an angel of the Lord spoke to him in a dream, this time telling him to flee from Herod into Egypt. Again, without even waiting for morning, Joseph chose to trust God and act. And after Herod's death, he once more acted in faith after hearing from God in his dreams. The remarkable thing is that because of Joseph's faith, God was able to use him to bring about the fulfillment of two other prophecies God had made to the whole world about his Son: that he would be called out of Egypt (Hosea 11:1) and that he would be called a Nazarene (Matthew 2:23). So Joseph's actions not only protected his wife and adopted son but also paved the way for God to ful-

fill prophecies spoken hundreds of years earlier.

We all know that things don't always go according to our plans. Sometimes, as happened to Joseph, God himself will make it clear that you are to make a course correction. Joseph teaches us that when that happens, the right response is to trust God and obey. When we do, he will not only bless us but also use us to fulfill his perfect plan for the world.

*Heavenly Father, thank you for Joseph's example of faith in action. Make us so attuned to you that we, too, will hear your voice. Strengthen our faith so we will be ready to act without hesitation and do our part in your perfect plan.*

## Trust

Divide the family into teams. Blindfold one member of each team and give the blindfolded player a nonbreakable Christmas tree ornament. Starting on the opposite end of the house or room from your Christmas tree, have a team guide the blindfolded player through the house to the tree using only their voices. (Don't try to navigate stairs blindfolded, and make sure that any hazards like stairways or sharp edges are blocked off before the blindfolded player begins.) Teams can go one at a time or race to see who gets their ornament hung on the tree first.

How did it feel to have to follow directions blindly? Were your teammates giving you trustworthy advice? God's voice will never lead you into a wall!

# Stay Tuned

## MATTHEW 1:18-25

*Over the past century,* the world has witnessed the most amazing technological advances in all of history, advances that have forever changed the way we live. Perhaps no invention in the past hundred years has had a greater impact on civilization than the radio. For the first time, there was a way to communicate with millions of people at once, even from thousands of miles away. Nearly every home in America had a radio, and as more and more networks competed for listeners, the words "Don't touch that dial!" were frequently heard between programs, encouraging listeners not to change the station during the commercial break but to hang on for a few more minutes to hear whatever exciting show was up next.

Today, we understand why those networks were concerned that people would change the station so quickly. Our society has a really short attention span! If we don't like one show, there are ten others to try; if things aren't working out with one spouse, we feel increasingly free to cut our losses and try again with someone else. This short attention span can have devastating consequences in our spiritual life. When life is hard and God doesn't seem to be doing anything about it, the temptation to "turn the dial" away from God and from his word can be overwhelming.

Joseph had a moment of temptation just like this. We're told he was a "just man," a description that means he was a student of the Hebrew Scriptures.

Suddenly, this righteous, godly man found himself betrothed to a girl who was pregnant with someone else's baby. Joseph was ready to "change the station" on this program. Matthew tells us that Joseph had made up his mind to break his engagement, but God spoke to him out of the blue, telling him that Mary's baby was from the Holy Spirit and that he shouldn't be afraid to marry her. In other words, God told him, "Don't touch that dial!"

Now, we might think God could have saved Joseph some time and worry simply by giving Joseph a little advance notice. Instead, God didn't speak up until Joseph had concluded that there was nothing to do but "change channels" on his life. I believe God sometimes waits to speak in order to toughen our faith and strengthen our dependence on him. The time Joseph must have spent praying to God for wisdom surely drew him closer to God and strengthened his faith, even if God chose not to answer right away.

Joseph hadn't planned on raising a baby that wasn't his. But because he didn't "change the station," he became the earthly father of the Son of God. When life is hard and you are thinking about giving up—on the church, on a relationship, on prayer, on God, or on yourself—don't touch that dial. God still speaks at exactly the right moment to keep us tuned in to him and his perfect plan for our lives. As Mary and Joseph would attest, we can be part of miraculous things when we stay tuned.

*Dear Father, help us to turn to you in times of doubt and fear. Strengthen our faith while we wait to hear from you, and give us patience to wait for your answers. Thank you for letting us hear from you at Christmas, and help us to stay tuned in to your plan for us this season and all year.*

## Narrate

Choose one person to begin telling a story. (You can make up your own or use the beginning of a familiar one, like Goldilocks or Red Riding Hood.) But tell only a little bit of the story, and then stop on a cliff-hanger or in a place that invites the next person to continue the story.

Did your story take some surprising turns? Did anyone know early on how it would end? When one author writes an entire story, it's likely to make much more sense. Who is writing the story of your life?

# Share Your Story

LUKE 1:68-79

***Can you imagine*** being one of the 12 people who walked on the moon? If I'd been part of something so amazing, something that so few people have experienced, you can bet I'd brag about it to everyone I met! When awesome things happen to us, it's natural to want to share the news with the people around us. You think the guy who went skydiving over the weekend keeps quiet on Monday? Or that someone who's climbed Everest just shrugs when asked if he likes hiking? No way! Incredible things fill us up until we can't contain our excitement any longer, and we just have to tell anyone who will listen.

When we look at the first Christmas, we see that those who encountered Jesus had the same reaction.

Mary was barely through the door of Elizabeth's house before she was pouring out her excitement over the child she carried. The shepherds told everyone they could find about the angels and the baby they had seen. And when Zechariah saw the miracle the angel had promised him, he immediately began to speak—he couldn't say enough about the goodness of God. His response shows us exactly how we, too, should respond to the amazing event we celebrate at Christmas.

Zechariah begins to "testify"—a word that means "bear witness" or "give evidence." A witness is someone who has seen something with their own eyes, who can offer proof from their own life that something is true. Zechariah testifies over and over of God's faithfulness to the nation of Israel and to him. Zechariah takes the witness stand and gives evidence that God is keeping the promise he made through Abraham and the prophets to send the world a Savior—and that God has kept his promise to give Zechariah and Elizabeth a child.

Zechariah has also personally experienced God's goodness and love—the fulfillment of God's promise "to give knowledge of salvation to his people in the forgiveness of their sins" (verse 77). He testifies that we can come to our God without fear and that he is coming—not in judgment, as we deserve, but with tender mercy, "to give light to those who sit in darkness and in the shadow of death" (verse 79). Zechariah's song is known as the Benedictus (from the Latin translation of the first two words, "Blessed be"). Zechariah has encountered God, and it's left him with nothing but good things to say.

In this season, many people try to conjure up warm and fuzzy feelings about Santa, and some feel let down when all the gifts have been opened. But we have real joy in our celebration because we, like Zechariah, know that God has kept his promise. We have experienced his love. Like Zechariah, we should be so overwhelmed by our experience of the Savior that we can't help but share the evidence with our friends and neighbors. We can witness that God keeps his promises, because we've seen it with our own eyes. We can witness that God offers forgiveness, because we've been forgiven. Every Christmas gives us an opportunity to testify to the love of God by sharing our story.

*Jesus, thank you for all the ways we've seen you in our lives, and for the way we experience Christmas because we know you. Help us to be so filled with amazement at what you've done for us that our excitement would spill over into our words and actions as we testify that you are love and that you are faithful. Amen.*

## Serve

Zechariah testified with his words, but we can also testify through our actions. The Christmas season is filled with opportunities to show others that God is love. Find a place where your family can serve others and show them the love of God. Take homemade cards to a nursing home, offering the residents company and friendship during a season that can be very lonely for them. Take decorations or gifts to a children's hospital, and ask how you can pray for some of the patients. Take some treats to your local police or fire station with a note of thanks and encouragement.

# O Little Town of Bethlehem

MICAH 5:2

*I once read an article* in a travel magazine that listed the best places in the world to see amazing architecture, taste exquisite food, and enjoy the arts and culture. The top of the list was filled with great cities like New York, Paris, Tokyo, and Sydney, and I can say from personal experience that yes, these cities are amazing places! But if I were making a list of the greatest cities in the world, I'd include one that most travel writers would laugh at—a little town in Israel called Bethlehem.

An ancient prophet named Micah first proclaimed that there was something special about this sleepy little town just outside of Jerusalem. It was known as the city of David because that's where he was born and was later anointed king over Israel. By the time Jesus was born, however, this was ancient history, and Israel had been under the rule of others for too long for anyone to care much about the birthplace of a long-ago king. But Micah put Bethlehem back on the map with his prophecy: "But you, O Bethlehem Ephrathah, who are too little to be among the clans of Judah, from you shall come forth for me one who is to be ruler in Israel, whose coming forth is from of old, from ancient days" (Micah 5:2).

This prophecy is one of the clearest and most direct prophecies of the Messiah in the entire Bible, and it was made more than 700 years before Jesus was born. To put this in perspective, imagine someone asserting in the year 982, 750 years before George Washington was born, "From Mount Vernon, Virginia, will come the first president of the United States"!

God used Micah to put on record that the one who would be born in Bethlehem would not only rule over Israel, but would be God in the flesh, "whose coming forth is from of old, from ancient days." The Hebrew word for "ancient days" literally means "days of eternity." In other words, the Messiah was going to come from eternity to a specific spot on earth, fully human, with a birthplace just like everyone else. Micah's words exist as proof for us that God keeps his promises—that the birth in Bethlehem wasn't an accident or a last-minute decision, but was in God's plan for centuries.

Micah tells us specifically that Jesus would come from Bethlehem Ephrathah. In Micah's time, the city actually had two names—Bethlehem, which means "house of bread," and Ephrathah, which means "fields of fruit," referring to vineyards. The fact that Micah uses both names is not a coincidence.

God knew the associations we would make between bread and wine and Christ's body and blood, and he made sure that even the name of the city the Savior would come from would point people toward his plan for salvation. Bethlehem may have been just a little town, but at the first Christmas, God used it in some pretty big ways—as the birthplace of the King and a signpost for salvation.

*Father God, your attention to detail amazes us. We are encouraged by your faithfulness to fulfill prophecy, and we are humbled by the care you took to point us toward salvation. Let the town of Bethlehem be a reminder to us of your love and power as we celebrate Christmas. Amen.*

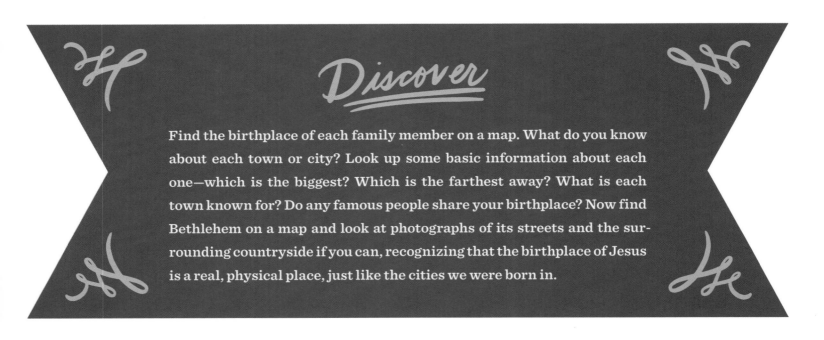

## Discover

Find the birthplace of each family member on a map. What do you know about each town or city? Look up some basic information about each one—which is the biggest? Which is the farthest away? What is each town known for? Do any famous people share your birthplace? Now find Bethlehem on a map and look at photographs of its streets and the surrounding countryside if you can, recognizing that the birthplace of Jesus is a real, physical place, just like the cities we were born in.

# Away in a Manger

LUKE 2:1-7

*"Away in a manger,* no crib for a bed, the little Lord Jesus lay down his sweet head." This hymn was inspired by a single verse in the Bible that tells us that Jesus was laid in a manger "because there was no place for them in the inn." You're probably extremely familiar with this part of the Christmas story, but it's easy to get the wrong idea about Christ's birth from this simple line.

If someone today is traveling and finds himself without a place to stay, we usually assume he didn't plan his trip very well—he should have made a reservation beforehand! But far from being an accident or a sign of poor planning, Jesus being laid in the manger is actually the result of a plan so detailed and so amazing, only God could have brought it about.

In order to understand how Jesus came to be laid in a manger, we have to understand why he was born in Bethlehem at all. Caesar Augustus had decided to take a census of everyone in the Roman Empire—including Jews who were not even Roman citizens. Rome was expanding so quickly, a tally had to be taken to make sure everyone was being taxed correctly so the empire would have the money it needed to operate. Scholars tell us this was the first census ever taken in the Roman Empire, and the timing of Caesar's decree was such that Joseph and Mary would be in the town of Bethlehem—not on the road, not already back home—when the time came for Jesus to be born.

Caesar Augustus surely thought the decree was his idea and the timing was up to him. But it turns out that he was just running an errand for God. You see, 750 years earlier, God had revealed through the prophet Micah that his Son, the Messiah, would be born in Bethlehem (Micah 5:2). Because God is in complete control and knows everything, he knew that Caesar would make the decree at just the right time for Mary and Joseph to be in Bethlehem for Jesus's birth and for Micah's prophecy to be fulfilled.

If God knew exactly when and where Jesus would be born, then we can safely assume that he also knew that after Jesus's birth, he would be laid in a manger because there was no room at the inn. God didn't forget to make a reservation for Jesus. Far from being a mistake or an oversight on God's part, the fact that there was no room at the inn was a preview of how the world would reject him and how people would shut their hearts and their lives to him.

The things you see happening every day may appear to be accidental, coincidental, or unimportant, but the story of Jesus in the manger reminds us that nothing is accidental. God is directing all of it to accomplish his plans. As you celebrate this often hectic and stressful season, remember that God hasn't overlooked a single detail.

*Dear Lord, thank you that you oversee every tiny detail of our lives, from what we will eat to where we will sleep each night. Help us to trust you when our future feels uncertain and to look for your hand at work whenever life feels random and out of control. Amen.*

## Help

If you had just arrived as a guest in your city and all the hotels were full, where would you go? Would you stay with friends or family? What if you didn't know anyone in town? Would you look for a store or restaurant that was open all night? What about a bus station or airport?

The next time your family is in a public place, imagine staying there all night. What would it be like? Before you go home, pick up some personal hygiene items (wet wipes, toothbrushes and toothpaste, deodorant) and nonperishable snacks and drop them off (along with a cash donation if you can) at your local homeless shelter or halfway house to help families with no other place to stay.

# Three for the Price of One

## LUKE 2:8-14

*I've always loved* a good bargain. If I'm out shopping and a sign tells me I can get "three for the price of one," I'm going to stop and look, and if it's really a good deal, there's a good chance I'll be buying three even if I didn't need one in the first place!

We've heard many times that Jesus is the best gift of all, and while that's absolutely true, it's easy for those words to start to sound a little cliché and for us to become desensitized to just how true they are. When I think of the gift of Jesus, I remind myself that He's not just one gift, but "three for the price of one." One of the most well-known Christmas songs of all time, "Hark! the Herald Angels Sing," perfectly summarizes the three gifts that Jesus brought to the world when he was born.

*"Joyful, all ye nations rise."*

The first gift Jesus brought was joy. Anyone who's ever celebrated a new baby understands the joy that surrounds the birth of a new life, and Jesus's birth was no different. The angel immediately proclaimed "good news of great joy"—and not just for his mother and father. All people everywhere would experience great joy because of his birth. That tells us a lot about the kind of Father God is to us. Yes, God cares about our righteousness, but he also desperately wants to offer us real, lasting joy—the kind that can't be jeopardized by changes in our economic status, employment, possessions, or relationships.

*"God and sinners reconciled."*

The second gift the angel announces is hope.

"Unto you is born this day in the city of David a Savior, who is Christ the Lord." To a world of sinners, doomed since Eden to die for our sins, a Savior has come. No longer do we need to fear death; no longer does our sin have to separate us from the God who loves us. He has made a way for us to be reconciled with him—he has sent a Savior.

*"Peace on earth and mercy mild."*

Finally, the angel is joined by a vast number of heavenly messengers who sing, "Glory to God in the highest, and on earth peace." In the current age of conflict and violence, peace may feel like a foreign concept. We wince every day when we turn on the news, afraid of what new attack or threat we'll hear about. When Jesus came, he brought the internal peace of knowing we are loved by God and reconciled to him. He also brought hope for peace with the world around us as we respond to violence by sharing the lasting peace we've found in Christ.

The angel wasn't just making a birth announcement, but advertising an unbelievable three-in-one gift of joy, hope, and peace, given by God to anyone who wants it. When we receive Jesus, we're receiving everything we could ever want, and that's why he is truly the best gift of all.

*Father God, thank you for the incredible gift you gave us in your Son, and thank you for the gifts of joy, hope, and peace found in him. May our joy this season remind us that you are a good Father. Help us to be mindful of the hope for salvation we have in Jesus. And help us to find ways to share the peace we have in you with the world around us this Christmas. Amen.*

## Thank

The birth of Jesus gives us many gifts to be thankful for, and just as we want to acknowledge and appreciate every one, so we should also show our appreciation for the gifts we receive from friends and family. Purchase or create some Christmas-themed note cards and write some thank-you notes to some of the people in your life. Younger children can draw pictures of what they're thankful for, and parents or older siblings can add a note. Thank grandparents for their support and love in your lives, for coming to soccer games or choir concerts, or having your favorite snack when you visit. Thank teachers for the time they spend preparing lessons and the personal interest they take in each of their students. Thank church staff for their service and their leadership in your spiritual life.

# Joy to the World

LUKE 2:8-12

**"Joy to the World"** is one of my favorite Christmas carols. In fact, let's sing it right now: "Joy to the world, Santa Claus has come! Let us receive our gifts!"

What? That's not how it goes? That certainly seems to be the song a lot of people sing this time of year. It breaks my heart to see how this world tries to convince children and adults alike that Santa Claus is the reason Christmas is a joyful and happy time. No disrespect to the jolly old elf, but if his coming to town is the best reason someone can give me to celebrate Christmas, I might as well just forget the whole thing.

Don't get me wrong—there's nothing wrong with Santa or gifts or any of the other fun stories or traditions that have come to be part of Christmas. But those things bring temporary happiness at best. Christmas happiness is as far removed from Christmas joy as the North Pole is from Bethlehem. Christmas joy is for all people, not just those who can afford a pile of gifts. And Christmas joy lasts all year. As the song says, Christmas brings "joy to the world" because "the Lord is come."

There is a reason why Jesus Christ came in human flesh, the heavenly Son of an earthly mother. I think that Immanuel, "God with us," is one of the sweetest of God's many names. After Jesus came in the flesh, God was no longer "God above us" or "God separate from us," but rather, God who shares our grief, our hunger, and our pain. Wrapped in rags, placed in a feeding box for oxen, Jesus was like us—helpless as a baby, forsaken as an adult, and subject to death.

This is reason enough for joy. We worship a mighty, holy God who found a way to relate to us and who literally met us on our level. And yet there is an even more compelling reason to have joy at Christmas. When Jesus Christ came in his humanity, he was like us in every way except one—he had no sin—and so he could be the perfect sacrifice that would cancel our debt with God. This is the reason our Christmas joy beats any earthly gift or celebration. When the Lord came, he came not only to be with us but also to be our Savior, just as the angels told the shepherds.

This is the best news we'll ever hear at Christmas. This is the joy behind all the warm fuzzies. This is the excitement behind every gift we unwrap. Unlike Santa, who vanishes into the night, Jesus is "God with us" forever. And unlike presents that break or are outgrown, the gift of salvation is eternal and brings eternal life. The best news you will ever hear at Christmas is not "Santa Claus is coming to town," but "the Lord is come." Joy to the world!

*God in heaven and with us, thank you that you left heaven to share our life on earth, and thank you that we, in turn, can share eternal life with you. May our joy during our Christmas celebrations and traditions be rooted in you, and may every fun story and activity of this season point us back to you.*

## Draw

On a large piece of paper (use craft or butcher paper, or tape several smaller pieces of paper together), draw the outline of a Christmas tree. Using markers or crayons, have every member of the family write or draw their favorite things about Christmas on the body of the tree, where the ornaments and lights would go. Include favorite holiday foods, movies, songs, books, and so on. At the top of the tree, where the star or angel would go, write "Jesus" as a reminder that all the other pieces of our Christmas celebration point to him as the best part.

# Party like the Shepherds

LUKE 2:8-20

*Christmas is not only* my favorite holiday, it's my favorite day of the entire year. My whole family gets together to exchange gifts, laugh, joke, eat…it doesn't get better than that!

December 26 is a different story. The presents have all been unwrapped, most of the pie has been eaten, and I have to start thinking about packing away the decorations and going back to work. Every year, I am amazed that I can go from so happy to so bummed out just one day after all that "joy to the world." I think the problem could be that I was *celebrating* Christmas without *experiencing* Christmas. What's the difference? For the answer to that, let's look at some of the first folks to both celebrate and experience Christmas—the shepherds.

Today, if you're in advertising and you want to get the word out about something, you try to get the right people talking about it. If an Olympic athlete or chart-topping singer mentions your product or event, people pay attention. When God wanted to get the news out about Jesus's birth, he used angels to send a press release to a select group of people.

By today's rules, those people should have been influential, popular, and well-respected so that when they started talking about this new baby, people would listen. Instead, God leaked the news to shepherds—people on one of the lowest rungs of the social ladder. Uneducated, unskilled, and usually unwashed, shepherds weren't even allowed to testify in court because their word wasn't considered trustworthy. When they got the news about the Savior, however, these rough, dirty rejects celebrated in a way that set an example for all of us.

These guys experienced Christmas firsthand. They were there that night and saw the stable, smelled the animals, and heard the baby cry. After their experience, they told anyone who would listen about what they had seen and heard. Once we've experienced firsthand the reality of God made flesh, once we've seen the baby for who he is, we, like the shepherds, can't stay silent. Our witness should be the first element of our celebration. The reason for all the cookie baking and carol singing should be our desire to break the news to the whole world that God has come to earth.

Our experience of Christmas changes the heart behind our celebration. The joy we have because of this news and our desire to share it doesn't fade when the cookies have all been eaten. The ways we witness after Christmas might change, but the joy behind our message is unfading.

The shepherds celebrated Christmas not only by sharing the news but also by worshipping. God is just as worthy of our worship on December 26, March 3, and July 12 as he is on December 25. We don't keep the nativity scene up year-round, but the memory of the baby in the manger should kindle in us the spark of worship even after the decorations have been packed away. In the end, if we celebrate Christmas as the shepherds did, we'll find that even among the crumbs and crumpled paper of December 26, our reason to celebrate, to witness, and to worship is with us every day of the year.

*Father God, make us more like the shepherds. Help us to see the baby in the manger as the Savior he is. Let our celebration be driven by witness to others about our experience and the impulse to worship you, and let the spirit of this celebration stay alive in our hearts all year long. Amen.*

## Celebrate

Pick a few dates on the calendar for some "bonus Christmases" this year. When those dates arrive, find some little ways to celebrate Christmas in every season. Create a "bonus Christmas" box to store a few Christmas paper plates, a little Christmas candy, and a pretty holiday dish or candle. Make a CD of all your family's favorite Christmas songs to sing during your bonus Christmas. Buy an extra box of inexpensive Christmas cards from the dollar store and send them out later in the year—you can even write in them now and save them to send when your bonus Christmas dates arrive!

# Paul's Christmas Story

PHILIPPIANS 2:5-11

***One of the best-loved*** and most familiar Christmas stories (besides the actual Christmas story) is Charles Dickens' masterpiece, *A Christmas Carol*. It's been made into a stage play, a West End musical, and at least 19 different film versions, not counting the dozen or so spoofs and modern retellings of the story. Nineteen movie versions of the same story might seem a little redundant, but the story is such a powerful and touching one that you can get something new out of it almost every time you see or read it.

There are multiple "versions" of the Christmas story in the Bible as well. Matthew's and Luke's accounts of the birth of Jesus are the most famous, probably because they offer the most detail, making it easier to picture the events of the birth and the people involved. But the apostle Paul actually gives an account of the birth of Jesus as well, though it's not immediately obvious as such. He never uses the word "baby," and he never mentions Mary or Joseph, the stable, or the shepherds, so at first glance it looks nothing like the Christmas story we're so familiar with. When we look closer at Paul's Christmas story, however, we see what's going on—Matthew's and Luke's versions answer the who, what, when, and where of Christmas, and Paul's version answers the how and the why.

Matthew and Luke don't use any fancy theological language when talking about the baby Jesus—they're describing the human baby born to Mary, and that's how they talk about him. Paul, on the other hand, starts off his Christmas story by explaining perhaps the most mysterious and miraculous thing about Christmas: At the same time the baby Jesus was fully human, he was also fully God.

When Paul ways Jesus "was in the form of God" (Philippians 2:6), he's using language that referred to the Roman practice of using wax seals and signet rings. A signet ring was used to press a distinctive emblem or mark into hot wax to create an exact representation of the mark on the ring, and any letter or order bearing the seal had as much authority as the person wearing the ring. Paul tells us that Jesus was the exact representation of God when he came to earth, not giving up any of his deity or authority, but he was also fully man. In the Incarnation, he was "taking the form of a servant, being born in the likeness of men. And being found in human form, he humbled himself" (verses 7-8). He was the exact representation of man as well as God.

This truth, that Jesus was both fully God and fully man, is at the root of the how and why of Christmas. How could a human baby eventually become the perfect, sinless sacrifice for our sins? By being fully God throughout his earthly life. Why would Jesus take on the assignment of living as a human and taking on suffering and death? Because he was the only one who could. Only a Savior who was fully God could live a sinless life; only a Savior who was fully human could die. On that holy Christmas night, a Savior was born who was both.

*Lord God, it is a mystery and a miracle that you came as fully God and fully man, but because you did, we can be fully forgiven for our sin and fully accepted by you. May our hearts be touched by the Christmas story each time we hear it this season, and may our eyes be opened to see more and more of the wonder of the birth of Jesus. Amen.*

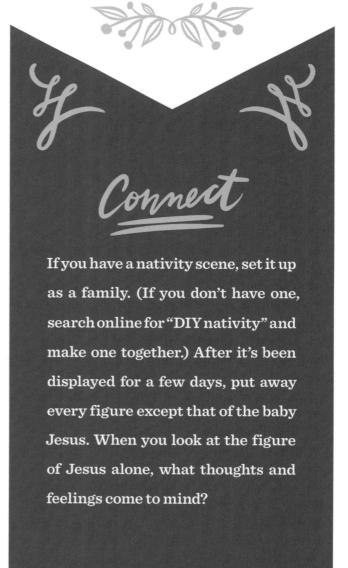

## Connect

If you have a nativity scene, set it up as a family. (If you don't have one, search online for "DIY nativity" and make one together.) After it's been displayed for a few days, put away every figure except that of the baby Jesus. When you look at the figure of Jesus alone, what thoughts and feelings come to mind?

# God's Christmas List

JOHN 3:16

**When you hear the** words "Christmas list," what do you think of?

When I was a kid, the only Christmas list I worried about was the list of things I wanted to get for Christmas. I was afraid that if I didn't tell everyone what I wanted, I'd end up getting a bunch of socks and underwear!

As an adult, my Christmas list shows the gifts I plan to buy for other people. If you have a list like this, who's on it? Probably your family members and closest friends, and maybe some teachers or coworkers. God has a Christmas list too, the longest in history, and the Bible verse that tells us about it is the most famous verse in the Bible: "For God so loved the world, that he gave his only Son, that whoever believes in him should

not perish but have eternal life" (John 3:16).

You can see what makes God's Christmas list so long—"God so loved the *world*." Unlike another famous Christmas list, God's list isn't based on whether you've been naughty or nice. Are you in the world? Then you made his list. God never made a person he didn't love unconditionally, and just as we put our loved ones' names on our Christmas list, he put our names on his.

Of course, this isn't because we're so incredibly lovable—it's because God *is* love. That means that God's love has nothing to do with who we are and everything to do with who he is. Other people may love you because of what you do for them, or how you look to them, or who you are to them, but God loves you because he himself *is* love. This means we can't do anything to earn his love, and we can't do anything to lose it.

You may have been warned as a child, "You'd better be good, or Santa won't bring you anything but a lump of coal!" In contrast to that, I want to remind you that there is nothing you can do to lose your place on God's list. You can't do something so good it will make God love you more than he does right now, and you can't do something so bad that it will make God love you less. If all the people God loves are on his Christmas list, that includes you, and you're on it for good.

The second part of the verse tells us what God gave to every person on his list at Christmas—"he gave his only Son." When we make our Christmas list, we sometimes struggle to think of the perfect gift for each person. But God didn't have to look any further than his only Son for the literally perfect gift for each one of us—his sinless Son, who offers eternal life. The moment you believe that the baby laid in the manger 2,000 years ago was the Son of God and you give him your heart, you receive God's gift of eternal life, the gift he picked out just for you when he made his Christmas list.

*God, thank you for putting us all on your Christmas list. Thank you that your love and not our good behavior is the standard for making the list, and thank you for picking out the perfect gift for us in your Son. Amen.*

## Pray

Have everyone in the family make a list of the people they would like to buy gifts for. This list is theoretical, so you don't need to limit it! Discuss which gift you would buy for each person if you had unlimited money. How do those fantastic gifts compare with God's gift of his Son? Use your Christmas list as a prayer list for the rest of Advent, praying that each person would see Jesus in your life and be drawn even closer to him this Christmas.

# Christmas Is Coming

***When you think*** about the first Christmas, what names come to mind? Jesus, of course, and Mary and Joseph, and if you want to get really creative, you could include Caesar Augustus, since his name appears at the beginning of Luke 2. These are certainly the most familiar names from the first Christmas, but later in the chapter, we read about a less well-known man who happens to have a lot in common with us.

"Now there was a man in Jerusalem, whose name was Simeon, and this man was righteous and devout, waiting for the consolation of Israel, and the Holy Spirit was upon him. And it had been revealed to him by the Holy Spirit that he would not see death before he had seen the Lord's Christ" (Luke 2:25-26).

This time of year, the signs that something wonderful is on the way are everywhere. All around the neighborhood, people string lights and hang wreaths while carols play on the radio and bells jingle on street corners. In your own house, you might be making special holiday foods or arranging treasured decorations, and interesting packages may be appearing under the tree. With all these signs pointing to the approaching holiday, it's no wonder excitement is at an all-time high, especially for kids!

When my own sons were little, they would ask daily, "How much longer till Christmas? How many more days, Daddy?" Does that sound familiar? The closer it gets to Christmas, and the more signs we see that it's coming, the harder it can be to wait, as any parent who's ever been awakened at 3:00 Christmas morning knows!

Simeon knew a thing or two about waiting. We're not told much about him, but we know that he had been waiting a *long* time for Jesus. And not just waiting, but waiting with expectation, with absolute faith that what he was waiting for would come to pass. You see, God had promised Simeon that he would not die before he had seen the Messiah. So Simeon wasn't just *hoping* to see Jesus; he *knew* he would because he knew God is faithful. Just as we know that all the lights and decorations mean Christmas is coming, Simeon knew that God's promise meant a Savior was coming, and so

he looked for him eagerly.

Month after month, year after year, maybe even decade after decade, Simeon woke up every morning with Christmas-level excitement, thinking each day could be the one when God would fulfill his promise. Can you imagine waiting for so long with that kind of anticipation? It makes our wait for Christmas feel pretty insignificant!

Just as our wait for Christmas won't last forever, Simeon's wait ended when the Holy Spirit led him to the temple and he finally saw Jesus. We learn from Simeon to wait eagerly for Jesus, to look for him every day with the expectation that we will see him and be shown ways to serve him and glorify him.

*Dear Father, thank you for the fun of this season and for the anticipation that surrounds it. Make us like Simeon—eagerly watching for the signs of your presence in our daily lives and willing to be used by you. Thank you for being faithful to keep your promise to us to send a Savior. May our excitement for the celebration of his birth touch those in our lives who don't know you. Amen.*

# Draw

Give each member of the family some blank pieces of paper and a pencil. Draw pictures of as many of your favorite signs of Christmas as you can in five minutes. When time is up, share your drawings with each other. Who listed the most signs of Christmas? What was the most common sign? What was the most unique sign?

# Star of Wonder

MATTHEW 2:9-10

***According to the best*** guess of astronomers, there are a total of one billion trillion stars in the universe. *One billion trillion!* That doesn't even sound like a real number! That's a one with 21 zeros after it. There are giant stars, dying stars, and stars that burn blue or red or green. But perhaps the most famous and celebrated star in history is what's known as the Bethlehem star. I doubt whether any other object in the sky has been the subject of more conversation, study, or celebration than this star, especially at Christmastime.

There has been much speculation about what that star was. Some say it was a comet, and others say it was a supernova. One creative person said it was an angel with a big flashlight! Regardless of the scientific description of this star, it has been a "star of wonder" to billions throughout history, starting with visitors from the East 2,000 years ago.

The wise men, or "magi," as they were known, noticed something special about this star. They were experts in the stars and very familiar with the night sky, but the Bethlehem star was so unique, they followed it 550 miles from their homeland. A journey of this length by camel would have taken more than a month. They didn't have a map, an address, or even a name to help them find the one they were looking for. Strangers in a strange land, these wise men would have been hopelessly lost but for the light from the star.

Think about this: From the time those men left

their home, they couldn't see Jesus. They could only follow the light from the star that led them. If the star had gone dark halfway through their journey, they would have been helpless. If the star had simply refused to shine, they would never have found Jesus.

The number one job of that star was to be a light to lead people to Jesus. If you are a follower of Christ, that's your number one job too. "In the same way, let your light shine before others, that they may see your good works and give glory to your Father who is in heaven" (Matthew 5:16). We reflect the light of Jesus to the world in the way we live, act, and talk. The apostle Paul said it this way: "Be blameless and innocent, children of God without blemish in the midst of a crooked and twisted generation, among whom you shine as lights in the world" (Philippians 2:15).

Many of your friends and neighbors are helplessly and hopelessly lost because they can't see Jesus. If you refuse to shine, they might never find him. This Christmas, let your love and service shine to those around you so they will see your light and follow you to Jesus.

*Father God, thank you for letting us play a part in leading people to Jesus. Help us to shine brightly this Christmas in the way we treat others, in our words, and in our actions, and put us in the paths of those who are lost and wandering so they might see our light and follow us to Jesus. Amen.*

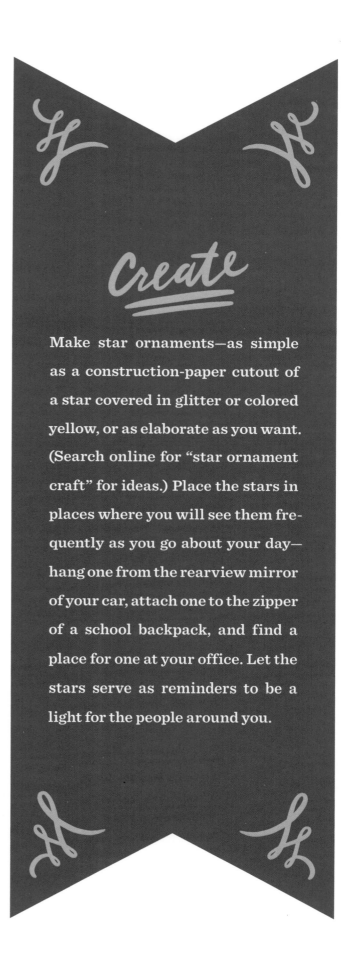

## Create

Make star ornaments—as simple as a construction-paper cutout of a star covered in glitter or colored yellow, or as elaborate as you want. (Search online for "star ornament craft" for ideas.) Place the stars in places where you will see them frequently as you go about your day—hang one from the rearview mirror of your car, attach one to the zipper of a school backpack, and find a place for one at your office. Let the stars serve as reminders to be a light for the people around you.

# Seeking Christmas

MATTHEW 2:1-11

**"We three kings** of Orient are bearing gifts we traverse afar." You're probably familiar with this popular Christmas song, and you might have noticed the several liberties it takes with the story of the wise men.

First, the Bible never tells us there were three wise men—just that they brought three gifts. There could have been two, or four, or ten visitors! Next, these men weren't kings, but scholars and stargazers known as magi, and they weren't from the Orient, but from Babylon, which is modern-day Iraq. They didn't even arrive at Christmas, but about two years after Jesus was born! So why did Matthew tell us their story? I think it's because the wise men teach us some important things about how God speaks to us, how he leads us, and what it means to be truly wise.

The first lesson we learn from the wise men is that if we want to find Jesus, we should start by looking in the word of God. This lesson is especially interesting because these men weren't believers in the Hebrew God when they started out. The magi were respected in their country because of their extensive knowledge of astronomy and their study of how the movements of the stars and planets related to events on earth. Babylon wasn't a Jewish nation, so these men didn't grow up following God's laws. Even so, when a star arose that they couldn't explain, these wisest of men turned to the Hebrew Scriptures for answers and chose to believe what they read there: "A star shall come out of Jacob, and a scepter shall rise out of Israel" (Numbers 24:17).

The wise men were looking for connections

between this new star and the kingdoms of earth, so finding this verse connecting a star with a "scepter" (a symbol for royalty) rising out of Israel would have been like hitting the jackpot. And though they hadn't been raised to revere Hebrew Scriptures or the Hebrew God, these wise men saw that God's word had been right about the star, so they chose to believe it was also right about a new king, and they set off to find him. When they got to Jerusalem and learned that the Scriptures named Bethlehem as the king's birthplace, these scholars again chose to believe the word of God and act on that belief.

As soon as the wise men made the decision to believe the word of God, God showed himself in an unmistakable way, causing the star to go before them until it stopped directly over the place where Jesus was. The wise men learned firsthand that believing God's word and acting on that belief guides us straight to Jesus. This is why the story of these magi is so relevant to you and me—every single day, whether we are believers or unbelievers, God wants to lead us to Jesus. We were put on this earth to seek Jesus, and when we believe God's word and follow his leading in our lives, we find him.

And just as God gave us his best gift at Christmas, so we, upon finding him, are to offer him our best—our worship and our treasure. That's what wise people do.

*Father God, you are the source of all wisdom and all knowledge. Without you, the wise men never would have found Jesus. Help us to follow their example by seeking Jesus in your word, believing your word to be true, and acting on our belief. Make us wise and lead us to Jesus every day of Advent and every day of the year. Amen.*

## Celebrate

If your nativity scene has wise men and camel figures, take these figures and place them far away from the nativity scene—after all, they're not supposed to arrive for about two years! Move them a little closer to the baby Jesus each day until January 6, when Epiphany, the holiday that celebrates the arrival of the wise men, is celebrated. Research some epiphany traditions online and choose one to celebrate as a family.

# A Bittersweet Holiday

## MATTHEW 2:11-12

**Dark chocolate is the** most frustrating candy ever made. It's sweet at first, but it leaves a bitter taste that I just don't care for.

At first glance, Christmas is a holiday that seems all sweet—fun times with loved ones, special music, pretty lights, good food, lots of presents…what's not to love? Even the biblical story of Christmas seems sweet to us—the new baby, the angels singing, and the star shining all paint a lovely picture. Yet all that sweetness leaves a hint of bitterness. The lights of the first Christmas cast the shadow of a cross.

This shadow appears in one of the "sweet" scenes we associate with the Christmas story—the visit of the wise men. If your family is like mine, opening gifts on Christmas morning is one of the sweetest parts of the holiday. Parents love to see their children's faces light up when they open that special toy they've been wishing for. Children love the fun of finally revealing secrets they've been keeping about what Dad bought for Mom or what they picked out for their siblings, and the room is full of excited squeals, thank-yous, and hugs. When the wise men gave their gifts, however, Jesus probably wasn't showing much excitement. Even though he was the Son of God, he was also human, and most human two-year-olds I've known are much more interested in the wrapping paper than the gift!

But what about his parents? Sure, Mary was probably pleased and honored by the first two gifts.

Gold was a gift for kings, and frankincense was used in offerings to God, so these gifts affirmed that her child was the Son of God, as the angel had said he would be. But when she saw the myrrh, she must have felt a bitter grief that would have seemed totally out of place for a birthday celebration. You see, myrrh was used to prepare the bodies of the dead for burial. When Mary saw it, it was a reminder that her baby had been born to die. From the moment she laid him in that manger on Christmas night, the shadow of the cross hung over Mary's baby.

And so we see that from the very first Christmas, the sweetness of the birth of Christ has been accompanied by the bitterness of what he was born to do for us on the cross. Far from making Christmas a sad occasion, however, the knowledge of why Jesus was born and what he would grow up to do makes the sweet parts of Christmas all the sweeter by comparison. If you try to separate the sweet from the bitter of Christmas, all you're left with is a cotton-candy holiday, one that tastes sweet for a second but has no substance and is unable to satisfy. The dark shadow of the cross makes the star seem brighter. And the final taste left on our tongues by Christmas is sweet, for we know the story doesn't end with the cross.

*Heavenly Father, we acknowledge the bitter parts of Christmas along with the sweet, and we recognize that it was to pay for our sinfulness that your Son was born to die. May the knowledge of the bitterness of Christmas stay with us throughout the season, helping us to appreciate the sweetness and giving meaning to our celebration. Amen.*

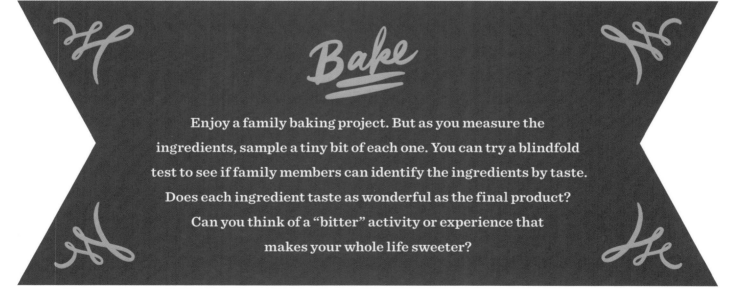

## Bake

Enjoy a family baking project. But as you measure the ingredients, sample a tiny bit of each one. You can try a blindfold test to see if family members can identify the ingredients by taste. Does each ingredient taste as wonderful as the final product? Can you think of a "bitter" activity or experience that makes your whole life sweeter?

# Exceeding Expectations

## GALATIANS 4:4-7

*A few years back,* an airline staged a promotional event in which an actor playing Santa asked passengers on a particular flight what they wanted for Christmas before they boarded their plane. Passengers laughed as they answered. One man joked that he hoped for socks, but others listed their dream gifts—big-screen TVs, jewelry, and toys. The surprise came when the plane reached its destination. Airline employees in that city had purchased and wrapped each passenger's Christmas wish. When the baggage carousel started up, hundreds of gifts poured onto the conveyor. As the passengers started to see their own names on the labels and realize what was happening, confusion turned to delight, and everyone was beaming as they opened their gifts. (Even the gentleman who asked for socks!)

The passengers probably would have been perfectly content simply to arrive safely at their destination. That was the airline's only legal obligation, and I'm sure that's what the passengers expected for their ticket price. That would have been enough, but in the spirit of Christmas, the airline went to great lengths not just to give each passenger a gift, but to surprise each one with the exact gift he or she wanted, far exceeding the customers' expectations.

God went infinitely further than this for us. The airline was obligated to at least transport the paying passengers, but God was under no obligation to rescue us from our sin and to ransom us from death. Thankfully, in his grace and unfailing mercy, he decided to send us a Savior, and if all we could expect from Jesus was that he would pay our debt and free us from sin, that would be more than enough. But he didn't stop there. Instead, we read that he sent his Son not only to redeem us but also to make us his adopted children. We who were sentenced to die for our sins weren't just pardoned—we were given an inheritance and the right to relate to God as *Abba*, or "Daddy," just as Jesus did.

It's hard to wrap our minds around just how much this adoption as God's children should amaze us. The Jews had been expecting a savior for thousands of years, but in all that time, they never dreamed that God would send his own Son to save them. They never expected the intimacy and privilege God would grant them through this Savior.

Jews rarely addressed God as Father—that seemed a bit too familiar for the holy Creator of the universe. Yet we are told not only that we are his children but also that God himself invites us to be on the same speaking terms with him that Jesus was—Jesus, who called him "Daddy" more than 200 times.

Adoption is always intentional. I've heard of unwanted or unplanned pregnancies, but I've never heard of an unwanted or unplanned adoption. People adopt because they want to, not because they have to. The miracle of Christmas is that God not only saved us but also chose us and adopted us as children and heirs. Just like his own Son, we too can call him "Father."

*Daddy in heaven, we are humbled and amazed that we can speak to you the way Jesus did and that you would call us your adopted children. Thank you not only for saving us, but for wanting and choosing us. Help us to no longer see ourselves as slaves but to fully embrace the freedom and love we find waiting for us as your sons and daughters. Amen.*

## Help

How can you show God's love to children waiting to be adopted or to families who have adopted? Consider supporting a child through an international relief organization and praying for that child as a family.

# He Wanted to Come

## COLOSSIANS 1:15-20

**When you were still** in the womb, did anyone ask you if you wanted to be born? Did they check with you to make sure you were okay with living the life that was waiting for you on the outside? Nope. You and I didn't have a choice when it came to being born. In fact, only one person in the history of mankind ever had a say in whether or not he would be born, and that was Jesus.

Unlike every other person who ever lived, Jesus was *born* but not *created*. The apostle Paul reminds us that Jesus was before all things, as timeless and eternal as God because he is God. "All things were created through him and for him" (Colossians 1:16)—that's definitely never been true of any other baby born on earth! Existing outside of time wasn't

the only characteristic Jesus shared with God. God is all-powerful, and so was Jesus—"In him all things hold together" (verse 17). God is all-knowing, so we can be positive that Jesus knew exactly what his life on earth would look like and exactly how it would end long before he was born as a baby.

Think about that for a second—Jesus, being one with the Father, knew exactly what was waiting for him in his life on earth. He knew every splinter and bruise he would have to suffer, he knew exactly how many people would mock him and abuse him, he knew he would have to watch people he loved die, and he knew he would be beaten and crucified. And yet Paul tells us, "In him all the fullness of God was *pleased* to dwell" (verse 19). Jesus didn't leave heaven and glory reluctantly or grudgingly. He was literally happy to do it—but why?

In the next breath, Paul goes on to explain that through Jesus, God was pleased "to reconcile to himself all things, whether on earth or in heaven, making peace by the blood of his cross." His love for us was such that he was literally happy to take on the pain and indignity of a human existence so we could be reconciled to him. When sin entered the world, mankind found itself reaching out for the God we had once walked hand in hand with, but no human being could come into his holy presence because of sin.

Because the fullness of God was pleased to dwell in Jesus Christ, he could do what no one else could. He could take the hand of God as God. He could take the hand of man as man, and he could place our hand back in God's, having covered our sins with his blood. In him all things hold together, and because of him, because he wanted to come, God and man can be together once more.

*Lord Jesus, thank you for coming to earth even though you knew about every hard thing that awaited you in this life. Thank you for being pleased to come anyway. Because of you, we can once more walk hand in hand with God. May we seek your presence this Christmas as you sought ours on Christmas 2000 years ago when you stepped out of eternity so we could enter it. You are the firstborn from among the dead and the firstborn over all creation, and we celebrate the night you came to the earth you created. Amen.*

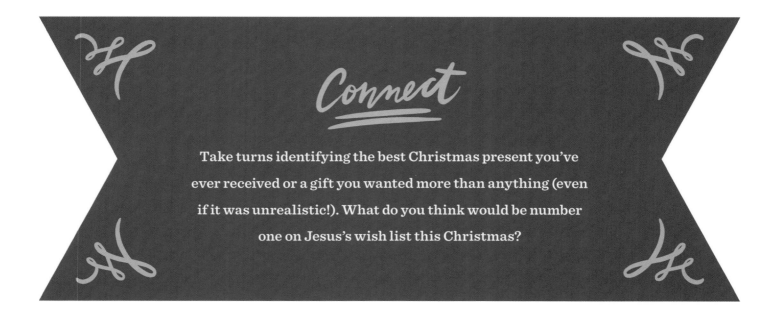

## Connect

Take turns identifying the best Christmas present you've ever received or a gift you wanted more than anything (even if it was unrealistic!). What do you think would be number one on Jesus's wish list this Christmas?

# The Most Beautiful Christmas Tree Ever

1 PETER 2:24

*Of all the traditions* and decorations associated with Christmas, the Christmas tree is one of the most loved. I'm willing to bet your Christmas tree is a big part of your celebration. Maybe you have a real tree that you picked out at a tree lot or even cut down yourself. Maybe you have an artificial tree, the kind that never turns brown or loses its needles. You might use colored lights or white lights, you might top it with a star or an angel, and maybe you decorate it while listening to favorite Christmas songs or drinking hot cider. It's hard to imagine celebrating Christmas without a beautifully decorated Christmas tree. But have you ever looked at your tree and wondered how the Christmas tree originated and whether it holds a deeper meaning than just lights and tinsel and decorations?

The custom of the Christmas tree began in Germany more than 1300 years ago, and it was originally called *Christbaum*, or "Christ tree." The first person in history to bring a Christmas tree inside may have been the great Christian Reformer Martin Luther, who noticed the stars shining through the branches of the trees as he walked one evening in the woods. In an effort to re-create the effect of stars in the trees for his children, he brought a Christmas tree inside and decorated it with small candles.

But as interesting as the history of our modern Christmas tree is, I believe the first real Christmas tree was found in Jerusalem, 2000 years ago, in the shape of a cross.

The cross of Jesus Christ is referred to over and over as a tree. In the New Testament, the word used to refer to the cross also means tree. The greatest description of that tree and what happened on it is found in one of the greatest single verses in all of the New Testament, 1 Peter 2:24: "He himself bore our sins in his body on the tree, that we might die to sin and live to righteousness. By his wounds you have been healed." The cross, made of the wood from a tree, ultimately became a reason for joy, just as a Christmas tree is a reason for joy.

Think about the shape of a Christmas tree—like an arrow, like a cross, it points up. Two thousand years ago, at the base of a tree stood a crowd of sinful people looking up. Just as lights hang on our tree, the Light of the world hung on that tree, pointing to a God who loves us so much that he sent his Son to die for us so that we might be saved.

Once a year, at Christmastime, we take a tree from outside our home and put it inside. That is exactly what God wants us to do in response to Jesus Christ on the cross—to invite him from outside our heart to live inside our heart, to live in the power he gives us to live for him and to do what is right. From now on, every time you see a Christmas tree, let it serve as a reminder to live your life for the One who came to give his life for you.

*Father, you have shown yourself to us in many beautiful ways, and the Christmas tree might be the most beautiful of all. Help us to keep that picture of you, the Light of the world, bright in our hearts all year. Help us to see you in every aspect of our celebration today, from the gifts to the good food to our love for our family. Thank you for the gift of Jesus, and let us not leave him under the tree, but accept him and invite him into our lives every day of the year. Happy birthday, Lord Jesus. Amen.*

## Celebrate

The waiting is over, and joy has come to the world! Plug in the lights, open the presents, play the music, eat the fudge! And when the day is over, gather as a family around the tree to thank Jesus for the gift of eternal life.

*For to us a child is born,*
*to us a son is given;*
*and the government shall be*
*upon his shoulder,*
*and his name shall be called*
*Wonderful Counselor, Mighty God,*
*Everlasting Father, Prince of Peace.*
*Of the increase of his*
*government and of peace*
*there will be no end.*

ISAIAH 9:6-7